Vietnam, 1970.

In an attempt to cut down on … turn, gain more support from a… popular opinion, the Nixon administration has secretly authorized the use of trained chimpanzees as surrogate soldiers in the Vietnam War. The project, headed by German twins Kurt and Klaus Heisler, was successful enough in the confines of the lab that the first all simian platoon of U.S. soldiers was fast-tracked into live action.

Kurt Heisler

Klaus Heisler

Government officials knew that for an idea as outlandish as this to gain public support, these initial missions in Vietnam would have to be an overwhelming success… They were, however, not.

Goliath

J.B.

Worzle

Faben

Pepe

Leakey

Goblin

The chimps, in a moment of challenged authority, lashed out against their military liaison and killed every human in their escort, including Klaus, one of the German twins. But despite finally being freed from their captors, the chimps have curiously continued to wage war against the Viet Cong, presumably still indoctrinated by their "experimental" training.

Clayton

After one such attack, the chimps came across a lone U.S. soldier, afraid and hiding from the advancing Vietnamese. Lost and posing no threat to the chimps, the young soldier was allowed to tag along with the chimps (mainly because he could light their cigarettes). With few other choices, the lost recruit tentatively followed along, uncertain where the chimps may lead him and unaware of the dangers they may bring.

Cap

Wyckoff

Clyde

Ed

Earl

John

After radio contact was lost with the platoon, the remaining twin quickly assembled a search and rescue team to track down the chimps, find out what happened, and keep the failed project from going public. To help track his prey, the German scientist, Kurt Heisler, also brought along a cast-off from the initial lab tests, a vicious baboon named Adolf.

Adolf

Tensions are rising as the days behind enemy lines continue to mount. The chimps and their pursuers have each taken casualties in recent V.C. attacks. To make matters worse, Adolf has disappeared, ditching Heisler to track down the chimps on his own… spurred on by amphetamines and a twisted sense of vengeance…

A light rain has begun to fall.

GUERILLAS™

VOLUME 3

by

BRAHM REVEL

designed by
KEITH WOOD
with
BRAHM REVEL
and
HILARY THOMPSON
edited by
CHARLIE CHU

AN ONI PRESS PUBLICATION

CHAPTER 7

"When elephants fight, it is the grass that suffers."
– African proverb

I dreamt about my Grandfather last night.

Which is weird, because I haven't thought about him in years.

I was only 7 when he died, so my memories of him are scattered at best.
WAAAAAAAA
And what I do remember feels like it's only partially accurate.

Like the gaps in my memories have been filled in with clips from old TV movies...
...and I can't tell what's real and what isn't anymore.

RINNGG!
HELLO?
My strongest memory of him is that he wanted me to call him "Pappy."

Said it was important.
WHAT?!

That it's what my Father called his dad.
KRAAK!
And what he called his Pappy before that.

Some kind of family tradition.

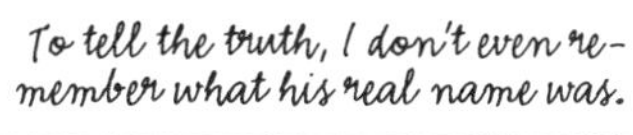
To tell the truth, I don't even re-
member what his real name was.

HONEY...
My Father never really talked
about him after he was gone.

A few months later
my Grandmother died.
ANOTHER DRINK, DEAR?

She was one of those women who
was lost without her husband.

SLAM!
I remember her
death even less.

Other details are vague.
Just snippets from the holidays, really.

Their house was uncomfortably hot. I remember that.
CAN'T WE LET THE KID OPEN ONE?!

GO AHEAD, BOY! I WON'T RAT YOU OUT!
The air, thick with bourbon and cigar smoke.

And no TV to distract from the awkwardness of our family gatherings.
THAT'S A JAP KILLER, BOY! JUST LIKE YOUR OLD MAN!
THE KID'S GOT A NAME, DAD.

He was a loud man.
COME HERE! WHAT DO YOU SAY?
Imposing in all ways, especially to a child.

When he would pick me up with his massive hands, he would grip me too tightly...
DAD, BE CAREFUL...
THANKS, GRANDPA.
...uncertain how to handle a child.

Or perhaps overcompensating for muscles that didn't work as well as they used to.
IT'S PAPPY, BOY! CALL ME PAPPY!

MARTHA!
THERE'S NOT ENOUGH BOOZE IN THE EGGNOG!
YES, DEAR.

UNGGH...

When it happened it was sudden...

His heart gave out while he was driving.

Died on impact.

They didn't bring me to the funeral, but I do remember the wake.

Our house felt so foreign with all those people in it.

It even smelled different.
Like a cafeteria at a hospital.

All bleach and lukewarm lasagna.
Everyone dressed in black...

Eating and chatting around a box with a dead man in it.
Even then it seemed absurd.

It was a closed casket.
Because of the crash.

But I knew he was in there...

Even in death, my Grandfather's cigar smoke smell was able to cut through the chrysanthemums and formaldehyde.

TING
TING
TING

I knew he was hiding

Too horrible to look at.
Desperately wanting to escape his fate.

And me...
...desperate for him to just go away.
CREEEEEE
To get out of my head...
To disappear forever...
BRAKKA!
BRAKKA!
BRAKKA!
BRAK

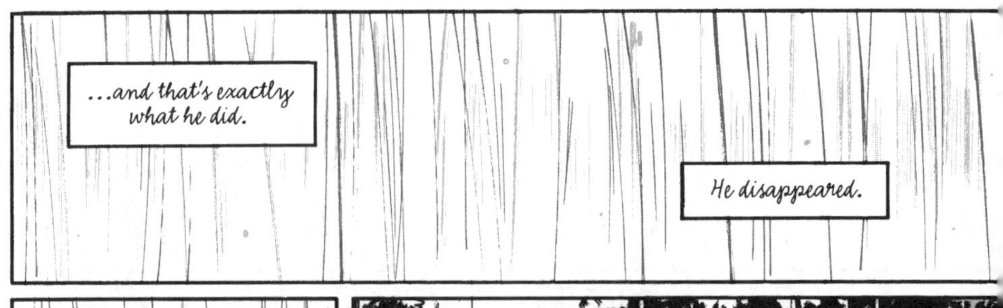
...and that's exactly what he did.
He disappeared.

And life went on without him.

Now, all that remains is a half forgotten memory...

...which fades a little more with each passing year.

I never mourned the loss of my Grandfather.
Never felt the need to say good-bye.

I guess it's because he was never really a part of my life.

He was just another stranger dressed in black.

Another ghost that would never haunt me.

I understand that now...

OOH?

WAAHH!

HUH
HUH HUH
HUH.

WUAA WAAH!
DUGGA DUGGA DUGGA!
HUH
HUH
HUH

In Basic, they told us that the Monsoon Season begins right before Thanksgiving...
I guess the holidays are coming...

ANYONE IN THERE? WE GOT THIS PLACE SURROUNDED!

WHERE IS THAT LITTLE GUY?

RIGHT HERE, MAN!

GO AHEAD... ASK IF THERE'S ANYONE IN THERE...

CÓ AI TRONG ĐÓ KHÔNG? BỌN TAO CÓ RẤT NHIỀU SÚNG NGOÀI NÀY!
MÀY SẼ CHẾT NẾU NHU VẪN TIẾP TỤC IM LẶNG!

I DON'T HEAR NOTHING...
YEAH... THANKS...
BUT I DON'T NEED TRANSLATIN' WHEN THEY DON'T SAY NOTHING...

EARL. CLYDE.
LET'S MAKE SURE THIS PLACE IS EMPTY...
MAYBE WE CAN HUNKER DOWN AND GET OUT OF THE RAIN FOR A FEW HOURS.

WHAT IS THIS PLACE?

THIS A OLD TEMPLE...
...NOT IN USE ANYMORE.
GEE... YA THINK?

WHO'S THAT?
THAT *SHIVA*...

...HE THE... DESTROYER.
SCARES THE LITTLE KIDS TO BE GOOD.

HEY!
I DON'T KNOW IF WE SHOULD BE IN HERE...

HE'S RIGHT, CAP...
WHY WE AIN'T CALLING IN AN EVAC? DON'T YOU THINK IT'S ABOUT TIME WE GET BACK TO BASE? WE GOT WOUNDED... P.O.W.S...
ALL IN DUE TIME, CLYDE.

CAP... SOME OF THEM OTHER CATS, FROM THE OTHER PLATOON, THEY STARTING TO GET ANTSY...
A LOT OF THEIR FRIENDS GOT--

I KNOW, CLYDE... WE ALL LOST PEOPLE WE CARE ABOUT.

OR DON'T YOU REMEMBER ED'S GUTS HANGING OUT FOR EVERYONE TO SEE...
I'M GETTING REAL SICK AND TIRED OF ALL THEM GOOD MEN DYING FOR NOTHING... IT *CAN'T* BE FOR NOTHING, CLYDE.

THOSE SUPPLIES OUT THERE WERE EITHER *COMING* FROM SOME-WHERE, OR *GOING* SOMEWHERE.
SOMEWHERE BIG...

...AND I INTEND TO MAKE THOSE *P.O.W.*S TELL ME WHERE THAT IS.

ALRIGHT, CAP.
I'LL CHILL THOSE FOOLS OUT. BUT THEY AIN'T GONNA STAY PATIENT FOREVER.
GOOD MAN.

LET'S GET THE SUPPLIES AND EVERYONE IN HERE AND OUT OF THE RAIN.

AND BRING THOSE DINKS INTO THIS BACK ROOM WHERE I CAN TALK TO 'EM.

OH...
UH... SORRY ABOUT THAT.

IT'S OKAY, MAN!
THEM DINKS NO FRIENDS OF MINE!

C'MON, YOU GRUNTS! LET'S MOVE IT! I AIN'T GOT ALL DAY! THE QUICKER YOU FLY, THE SOONER YOU'RE DRY!

ADOLF!
CAN YOU HEAR ME, ADOLF?

HEY, DOC...
IT'S PROBABLY NOT THE BEST IDEA TO BE SCREAMING OUR LOCATION OUT INTO THE BUSH.
FLIT

I KNOW, DOC... ADOLF'S A SMART MONKEY. THAT'S THE WAY YOU MADE HIM. HE'LL FIND US WHEN HE WANTS TO.
NOW, LET'S GET YOU OUT OF THIS RAIN.

EEEEEEEEEEE

EEE
KLUNK!
WAHH!

EEEEEEEE!
EEEEEEE!
EEEE

EEEEEEEE!
WAAAAH!!

WAAH!

drip...
drip...
drip...
drip...
Hooo

OOOH!

EEEEE
EEEEEE
AAAAA
AAAAA

WUA WAA!

WUH?

OOOH!
OOOH!

OOH!
OOH!

WUA!
OOOH!
OOH
HOO

WUH!
WAH!

HOO...
HOO...

NNG?

HOO?

WUAAA!
WAAAA!

URRRRNNN
EEEEE

EEEEE

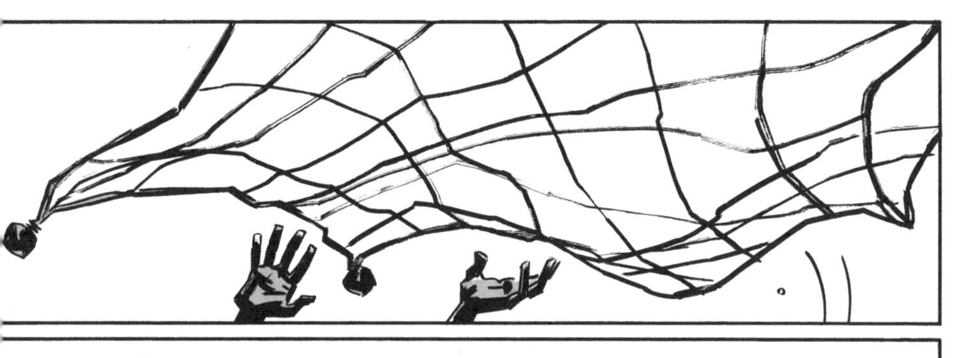

oof!

EEEE

EEEE

WAAA!

WUA!

WAAAAA

EEEK! BRRTT! BLAM!
EEEEE
EEE

CHUNK!
WIIIIRRRRRRRRRRRR

EEEK
CLANG!
CLANG!
CLANG!
CLANG!
EEEK
CLANG
EEEE
EEE

ANNT
ANNT
ANNT
KANG

ZZOOO

EEEEE
CLANG
CLANG
CLANG
ZIIROOSSH

CLANG!
EEEEE

CLICK!

GRRRRRR

RRRRR

RR

RAOW!

RAOW RAOW RAOW

EEEE!

WAH!
WAAAA

EEEE

THK

SPLASH

BAH!
HUH HUH

CKK

KKKKK

KKKKK

CHUNK!

PSH!
IT'S OKAY.
DON'T VURRY.
IT'S ALL GOING TO BE ALRIGHT NOW.

COME HERE, LITTLE ONE.
I WON'T HARM YOU...

JA! ZAT'S A GOOD BOY!
IT'S ALL OVER NOW.

VUD YOU LIKE A PRESENT? HERE'S A NICE HELMET TO KEEP YOU SAFE.

WE ARE GOING TO CALL YOU GOLIATH NOW.
YOU LIKE ZAT?
JA, I SINK ZIS IS A GOOD NAME...

...GOLIATH
IATH
GOLIATH
TCHK!
ALRIGHT, GUYS, WE'RE RUNNING LOW ON THESE...
...SO SAVOR 'EM, CUZ WHO KNOWS WHEN WE'RE GONNA FIND MORE.

YOU THINK GOLIATH WANTS ONE?

GOLIATH...?

WHERE IS HE?

WHAT THE HELL?

WHERE'D HE GO?

EVERYBODY SPEAD OUT AND LOOK FOR HIM! HE CAN'T HAVE GOTTEN FAR!

RRRRMMMMMMMMMMMBBBLLLLLL

WHERE ARE YOU, ADOLF...?
HOW COULD YOU ABANDON ME, TOO?

KRAK

WHERE WERE YOU TAKING THESE SUPPLIES?
GO AHEAD, ASK 'EM AGAIN...
MÀY ĐỊNH ĐEM CHỞ SÚNG NÀY ĐI ĐÂU? MÀY MUỐN LẠI BỊ ĐÁNH À?
ANSWER ME, DAMMIT!

KRAK!

CAP...
HEISLER...
YOU'RE NOT NEEDED HERE. I'D APPRECIATE IT IF YOU'D--
I CAN MAKE ZEM TALK FOR YOU...

...I CAN MAKE ZEM ALL TALK.
LEAVE, HEISLER...
LET'S BE HONEST, CAPTAIN... YOU ARE A GOOD MAN...
HONORABLE...
YOU HAFF TEMPORARILY LET YOUR HOT-BLOODED EMOTIONS GET ZE BEST OF YOU.
UND JA, YOU'VE ALLOWED YOURSELF TO BEAT ON ZEM FOR A LITTLE WHILE.

I'M IMPRESSED.
BUT WE BOTH KNOW YOU WON'T GO FAR ENOUGH TO GET ZE JOB DONE.
UND WE BOTH KNOW ZAT I VILL.
I CAN GET YOU ZE INFORMATION ZAT YOU WANT, BUT YOU MUST PROMISE ME WE VILL FINISH OUR MISSION...
...WE MUST FIND ZEM.

ED WAS RIGHT. THIS GUY'S A FUCKIN' *NAZI!*

IS ZAT VHAT HE THOUGHT?
NO, I AM NO NAZI.
I AM A MAN OF SCIENCE, NOT POLITICS.

POLITICS ARE A CLOUDY UND UNRELIABLE AFFAIR.
NO... VHAT I SEEK IS TRUTH!

UND I VILL NOT LET PETTY POLITICS STAND IN ZE WAY OF ZAT TRUTH.

SO VHAT'S IT GONNA BE, CAPTAIN?
TRUTH... OR POLITICS?

HEE!
HEE!
HEE!
HEE!

HEE! HEE HEE HEE HEE!

HEE HEE HEE
MÀY BỊ ĐIÊN VÌ CON KHỈ CỦA MÀY ĐÃ RỜI BỎ MÀY!

PFTTT!

WHAT?
WHAT'D SHE SAY?
SHE SAY HE JUST MAD CUZ HIS MONKEY GONE!

NÓ KHÔNG CÒN THUỘC VỀ MÀY NỮA, GIỜ NÓ THUỘC VỀ THẦN SHIVA!
HEE HEE HEE

SHE SAY HE NO LONGER BELONG TO YOU. HE BELONG TO SHIVA NOW!

LET ME START WITH HER!

BÂY GIỜ TẤT CẢ CHÚNG TA ĐỀU THUỘC VỀ THẦN SHIVA!
SHE SAY WE ALL BELONG TO--

ALRIGHT! THAT'S ENOUGH! SHUT HER UP AND GET HIM OUTTA HERE!

C'MON, DOC! LET'S GO...
YOU DON'T HAFF IT IN YOU, CAPTAIN!
ZIS IS ZE ONLY WAY!

CHRIST... IF HE AIN'T A NAZI, I'M SURE THEY'D HAVE HIM!

GOLIATH!
COME BACK!
WE NEED YOU!

. . .

RUMMMMMBBBLLLLL

ANYTHING...?
GOLIATH
0001
POSITIVE

THANK YOU...

WHAT CHOO GONNA DO WHEN YOU GET BACK?
BITCHES AND BREWS, MY MAN!
I HEARD THAT!
I'M JUST GONNA GET ON MY BIKE AND RIDE 'TIL I HIT THE OCEAN...

HMPF... PHILISTINES...

HEY, JOHN... YOU THINK I COULD CHECK OUT SOME OF YOUR MAGAZINES?
OF COURSE, MAN!
YEAH, EARL! CHECK 'EM OUT, THERE'S SOME GOOD STUFF IN THERE!

WHERE'S THE ONE ABOUT THEM NAZI BABOONS?
NOT SURE... BUT IT *IS* IN THERE! THEY'RE ALL GOOD, THOUGH.

HEY! SPEAK OF THE DEVIL! HOW'S IT GOING, DOC?
HMPF... MAY I SIT?
SURE, DOC! TAKE A LOAD OFF!

MEN

CIGARETTE?

NO, SANK YOU. I DON'T SMOKE.

WHY NOT?
JA, I HAFF BAD CONNOTATIONS WITH CIGARETTES...
...WE USED ZEM AS REWARDS FOR ZE CHIMPS DURING ZERE TRAINING...

...YOU KNOW, POSITIVE RE-INFORCEMENT...
...WHEN ZEY WOULD DO SOMESING GOOD, WE WOULD GIVE ZEM A CIGARETTE.

NAZI BABOONS
THEN WE ENGINEERED ZE CIGARETTES TO BE MORE ADDICTIVE, SO ZEY WOULDN'T JUST *WANT* ZEM...
...ZEY WOULD ***NEED*** ZEM.

UND IN TURN, ***ZIS*** MADE ZEM TRAIN HARDER. IT BECAME A VERY EFFECTIVE MEANS OF CONTROL FOR US.
BUT AS A RESULT, I SEE SMOKING ONLY AS A SIGN OF WEAKNESS.

THINK ABOUT IT... THE FIRST GUY TO SMOKE MUST HAVE LOOKED LIKE A GOD!

THIS GUY, PROMETHEUS, STOLE FIRE FROM ALL THE GODS UP ON MOUNT OLYMPUS...
...AND IT MADE IT SO HUMANS WERE, YOU KNOW, NOT SO DE-PENDENDENT ON THEM ANYMORE...
...LIKE THEY HAD SOME MAGIC OF THEIR OWN.
WELL, WHAT IF THESE FIRST CAVEMEN WHO SMOKED ALL THE WAY BACK THEN...
...WHAT IF THEY REALIZED THAT *THEY* COULD BE GODS, TOO?

THAT THEY HAD ALL THIS POTENTIAL IN THEM TO CREATE CITIES AND WARS, AND SUPER MONKEYS THAT SMOKE!

WHAT IF THE ACT OF SMOKING WAS THE SPARK THAT *TRULY* MADE US HUMAN?

...GODS AMONG BEASTS!
SO, WHAT D'YA THINK, DOC? AM I ON TO SOMETHING?

GODS AMONG BEASTS...
PERHAPS.
HONESTLY, I DON'T EVEN KNOW ANYMORE...

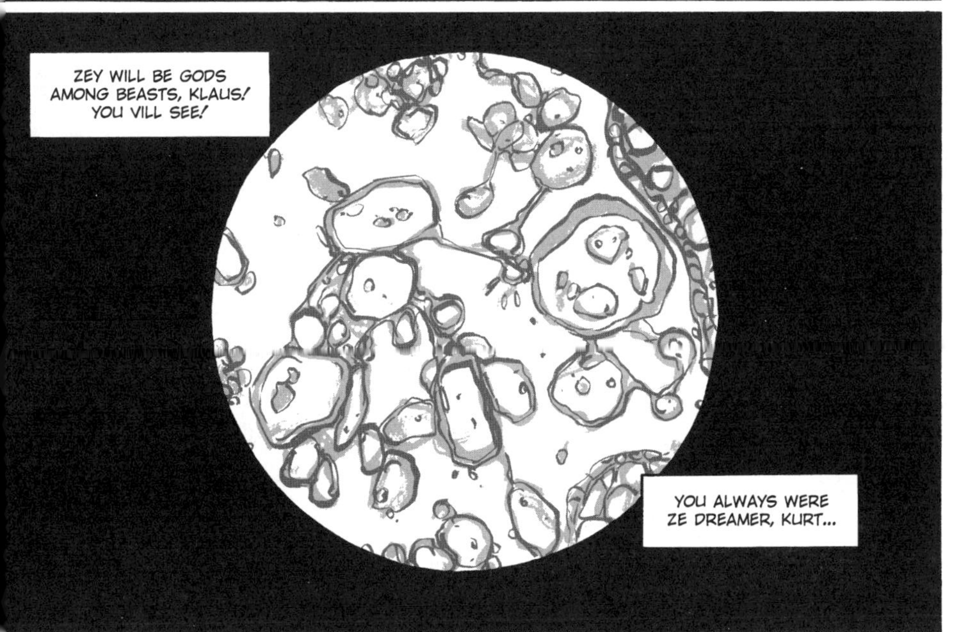
ZEY WILL BE GODS AMONG BEASTS, KLAUS! YOU VILL SEE!
YOU ALWAYS WERE ZE DREAMER, KURT...

...UND WHILE I AGREE ZAT ZE DIFFERENCE BETWEEN GOD, MAN, UND BEAST IS INDEED SLIM, IT IS IN FACT, US THAT ARE CHARGED WITH ZE ACT OF CREATION...
...SO, PERHAPS WE SHOULD LEAVE GENESIS TO ZE POETS OF OLD, JA?
ACH! YOU KNOW VHAT I MEAN, KLAUS!
YOU SOUND JUST LIKE ZE OLD MAN, BOTH DIS-MISSIVE UND SELF-AGGRANDIZING IN ZE SAME BREATH.
UND YOU ARE JUST AS STUBBORN!
BUT ADMIT IT, YOU CAN'T DENY HIS RESEARCH!
A BIT BARBARIC, WOULDN'T YOU SAY?
HUMANS ARE ZE PINNACLE OF ZIS RESEARCH, KURT... IF WE HAD ZE SAME ACCESS ZAT HE HAD, ZEY WOULD BE OUR SUBJECTS, TOO!
NO... I DISAGREE... ZE FRAGILITY OF ZE HUMAN MIND IS EXACTLY ZE REASON WHY WE ARE TASKED WITH CREATING AN ANIMAL SURROGATE!
WE MUST BE LOOKING FORWARD, NOT BACKWARD.

JA, PERHAPS... BUT AT ZIS STAGE, WE AREN'T JUST LOOKING FOR A SOLDIER, WE ARE ALSO LOOKING FOR A LEADER... AN *ALPHA!*
UND IT IS CHILDISH TO SINK ZAT WE WILL BE ABLE TO ACHIEVE ALL ZAT YOU ASPIRE TO WITHOUT A SUBJECT ZAT SHARES A MODICUM OF OUR OWN AWARENESS!
ALL I'M SAYING IS KEEP AN OPEN MIND, KLAUS... DON'T LET OUR FATHER'S FAILURES SKEW YOUR FINDINGS.
ZAT GOES BOTH WAYS, DEAR BRUZZER... MUSTN'T PUT ZE CART BEFORE ZE HORSE, JA?
HMPH... ZEN, PERHAPS IT'S BEST WE GET STARTED. HOW LONG HAFF ZEY BEEN IN ISOLATION?
FOUR WEEKS...
IS ZAT ENOUGH?
JA...
...I SINK ZEY SHOULD BE SUFFICIENTLY AMENABLE TO OUR SUGGESTION.
GOOD, ZEN LET'S BEGIN...

MP
Scope
Head Shot
Flank
P.O.W.
Friendly Fire
Sniper
Evac
Map
Click
Night
Day
Question
Ambush
Operation
Alpha
Omega
Booby Trap
Doctor
YES
Gook
VC
Storm
Valley
Rain
Jungle
Dustoff
Air Strike
LZ
Tunnel
Foxhole
Sky
Tree
Patrol
Bunk Down
Pungi Stick

Captain
Bouncing Bettiy
Smoke
Stream
Climb
Minute
Day
Stay
Go!
Base
Banana
Tea
Hike
Hour
Radio
Broken Arrow
NO
FUBAR
Take Cover
SNAFU
Retreat
Plan
Cross Fire
Divide
Surround
Search
Destroy
Reload
M-16
Frag
AK-47
Ammo
Machete
M-60
Collect

SO, KLAUS... VHAT ARE YOUR THOUGHTS ON ZE RECENT DATA SETS?
I DO NOT DISAGREE THAT ZEY ARE BOTH AMAZING SUBJECTS, KURT.
BOTH ARE EXTREMELY GIFTED PHYSICALLY.
ZEY ARE BOTH FAR STRONGER UND FAR FASTER ZAN ZERE HUMAN COUNTERPARTS...
BUT...?
BUT ZE BABOON SIMPLY DOESN'T HAFF ZE SAME MENTAL CAPABILITIES AS ZE CHIMPANZEE.
PERHAPS, BUT HE IS A BORN FIGHTER, KLAUS.
UND WE ARE CREATING SOLDIERS, NOT SCHOLARS.
...LET'S NOT CONFUSE THE TASK AT HAND!

UND YOU SHOULD NOT SIMPLIFY IT!
WE ARE NOT MAKING MINDLESS KILLING MACHINES, *KURT!*
WE NEED SUBJECTS WHO CAN NAVIGATE ZE FOG OF WAR!
BING!
ZEY MUST BE ABLE TO TELL ZE DIFFERENCE BETWEEN FRIEND UND FOE IN A CONFLICT WITH VERY FEW DISTINCTIONS.
UND WHAT ABOUT TACTICS?
STRATEGY?
ALL ARE COMPLEX DECISIONS BASED ON CONSTANTLY CHANGING VARIABLES.
FRANKLY, IT DISTURBS ME ZAT INTELLEGENCE IS NOT AN ATTRIBUTE ZAT YOU DEEM NECESSARY IN A SOLDIER.
1
2 3 6
5
4 9
1
2
3
5
A SOLDIER MUST KNOW ONLY HOW TO FIGHT, UND HOW TO FOLLOW ORDERS.
ANYSING MORE WILL ONLY RESULT IN CONFUSION.
ZIS HAS BEEN PROVEN COUNT-LESS TIMES.
YOU SEE, YOU ARE FOLLOWING A MODEL WHICH HAS ALREADY BEEN PROVEN UNRELIABLE.
MAKING AN ANIMAL MORE HUMAN TO BECOME A BETTER SOLDIER IS NON-SENSE!
WE HAFF ZE ABILITY TO CREATE SOMEZING NEW! SOMEZING DESIGNED SPECIFICALLY FOR ZE TASK AT HAND.
UND ZE BABOON HAS ALL OF THE RAW MATERIALS WITH NONE OF ZE DRAWBACKS!

EVER ZE DREAMER, KURT...
UND HOW DO YOU SINK YOU WILL ACCOMPLISH ZIS?
+
=
1
2
3
4
WE KEEP ZE VESSLE UND DISCARD VHATEVER WE CAN'T USE.
WE DELETE ZE CURRENT, UNPREDICTABLE PROGRAM UND START FROM SCRATCH.
IT WOULD BE RUDIMENTARY, BUT CONTROLLABLE.
YOUR HUBRIS IS DISCONCERTING, KURT.
4.1
11.1
8.7
DO YOU REALLY SINK YOU CAN ERASE WHAT A BILLION YEARS OF EVOLUTION HAS CREATED?
UND YOU, *KLAUS?* DO YOU REALLY SINK YOU CAN CONTROL IT?
ZEY ARE ANIMALS, KURT! ANIMALS!!! I COULD DO ZIS IN MY SLEEP!

MAN HAS BEEN CONTROLLING OTHER MEN FOR CENTURIES...
...YOU NEED ONLY LOOK TO ZE LAST GREAT WAR FOR EVIDENCE OF ZIS!
ADOLF
DOPAMINE
C8H11NO2 –
32 14 7 19
01-2
JA, UND LOOK HOW ZAT TURNED OUT! MAN IS NOTHING IF NOT UNPREDICTABLE.
NO, ZE SMARTER SOMESING IS, ZE EASIER IT IS TO CONTROL.
MAN WOULD BE EAISER ZAN ZE CHIMPS, JA! BUT ZE CHIMPS... ZEY WILL BE EASIER THAN YOUR BABOON.
YOU SEE, A SAVAGE MIND REACTS ONLY ON INSTINCT, WITHOUT THINKING...
BUT AN INTELLECT... AN INTELLECT CAN BE CONVINCED...
ADOLF
EVEN AGAINST ITS BETTER JUDGEMENT.

TAKE A LOOK AT YOURSELF, DEAR BRUZZER!
YOU PROFESS TO HATE OUR FATHER, BUT WHENEVER YOU OPEN YOUR MOUTH, IT IS HIS WORDS ZAT COME OUT!
"A SOLDIER MUST ONLY FIGHT UND FOLLOW ORDERS!"
LISTEN TO YOURSELF!
ME!?
I'M NOT ZE ONE TRYING TO RECREATE OUR FATHER'S OLD EXPERIMENTS!
ZIS ISN'T DACHAU, UND ZEY AREN'T HUMANS...
...ZEY ARE ANIMALS!
UND SHOULD BE TREATED AS SUCH!
A DOG CAN BE TRAINED, KLAUS...
...A MAN CAN ONLY BE TRICKED INTO THINKING HE'S RIGHT.

OH, YE OF LITTLE FAITH, KURT...

SCIENCE IS NOT ZE DOMAIN OF *FAITH, KLAUS!*
HELLO, ADOLF...

LOOK VHAT I HAFF FOR YOU...
JA... A CIGARETTE.

UND I HAFF SOMESING ELSE FOR YOU, TOO... SOMESING TO MAKE YOU FASTER, UND STRONGER... SMARTER EVEN.

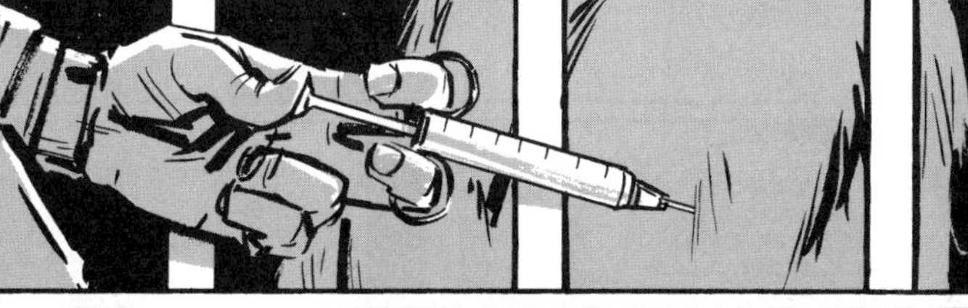
HE'S WRONG ABOUT YOU, ADOLF. ALL HE CARES ABOUT IS SUCCEEDING WHERE OUR FATHER FAILED.

BUT WHY BRAINWASH AN INTELLIGENT ANIMAL WHEN YOU CAN CREATE SOMESING ENTIRELY NEW...

...ACCELERATED EVOLUTION WITH A SINGULAR GOAL!

NEVERMIND WHAT KLAUS TOLD YOU! BRING HIM TO ZE M.K. WING. A LAB HAS ALREADY BEEN PREPARED.
YES, SIR!
WE WILL SEE WHO IS RIGHT IN ZE END? WON'T WE, BRUZZER?
JA, I SINK SO...

KRAACK!!!
RUMMMMMMMMMMMBBBBLLLLLL
KRACK!
RUMMMMMMMBBBELLLLL!

KRAK
Sniff
Sniff

KKRACKK!

RU MMMMBBLLLL

TSSSS...
SSS
SS SS

CLIP!
HEY!

EEEE
UMM...
UH...
IT'S YOUR TIME

CLICK!
IT'S YOUR TIME
TO BECOME
A MAN
-DA

CHKCH
IT'S YOUR TIME

KKKK KKKKKK

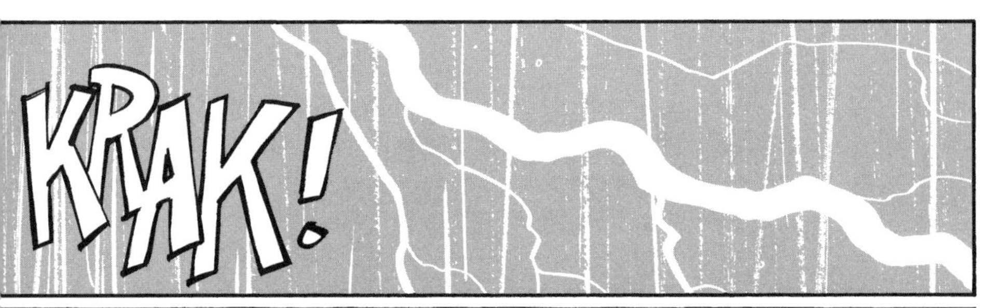
KRAK!

EEEEEEEEEEE

KA-KRAK!
ZZZZZZZ
RUMMMMMMBBLLLLL
Drip Drip
Drip

CLACK!
EEEEEE

THAT'S WHAT I SAID TO *HER!* I'M A *PERFORMER!*
AND DO YOU KNOW WHAT SHE HAD THE NERVE TO SAY TO ME?

"CLOWNS AIN'T PERFORMERS, THEY'RE JUST..."
"...THEY'RE JUST *CLOWNS!*"
NO...

SO WHAT'D YOU SAY?

WHAT COULD I SAY?
AFTER THAT, IT WAS OVER!

CLICK!
EEEE

THERE HE IS!
GET HIM!

CLANG!

BRAK
OH, SURE...

...I SUPPOSE YOU'VE BEEN HERE THE WHOLE NIGHT, EH?
...JUST LIKE ALWAYS...

....WELL THE JOKE'S ON YOU, "DR." WORZLE... CUZ YOU AIN'T MY PROBLEM NO MORE!
HE'S ALL YERS, DOC...

CHUNK

RRRRRRRR
WUH!
WUH!
WUHWAA

HAAAAA

HUH...
HUH
HUH...
HUH

HMPH!
WHU WHU
WUH
WAH!

WAAA

WA AAA

EEE

HOO HOO

HOOO

GRRN

WUAH!

WUAH

IT'S
KURT...
...JUST AS I HAFF PREDICTED.
ZEY'VE ACCEPTED HIM AS ZE *ALPHA.*
HMPH... FOR NOW...

NO, KURT... ZEY HAFF BEEN IMPRINTED.

ZIS IS WHO ZEY ARE NOW.

ZEY HAFF ACCEPTED IT. UND NOW, YOU MUST AS WELL.

WUH! WAAH!

POP!
POP!
THAP
BRAP!
WAAA
THAP
GOBLIN

BRA
PPP!

BRAPP
GOBLIN

GOBLIN

NEIN! NEIN! NEIN! NEIN! NEIN!
LEAKEY
WORZLE
GOBLIN

VHAT ARE YOU DOING?
YOU'RE ONLY MONKEYS, DON'T YOU UNDERSTAND?! YOU MUST USE *TEAMWORK* IF YOU EXPECT TO SURVIVE!
YOU MUST BE *DISCIPLINED!*
NOT LIKE ZIS!
ACH! ZIS IS USE-LESS.

NO! NOT *GOBLIN.*

HE MUST LEARN ZAT HIS ACTIONS HAFF CONSEQUENCES...

GOBLIN

CLAP!
CLAP!
WORZ

CLICK
WORZ

ZZZZZZZ
ZAP

IT SEEMS ZAT MY INSTRUCTIONS WERE UNCLEAR A MOMENT AGO...

...BUT NOW PERHAPS, ZEY ARE NOT.
JA?

IN HERE IS GOOD.
WORZLE'S GONNA HAVE A LITTLE TIME TO HIMSELF FOR AWHILE...
...MAYBE THINK ABOUT WHAT HE'S DONE, RIGHT?
WORZL

AH!
GOD-DAMMIT!

WHAT A PAIN IN THE ASS!

CLICK
C'MON, MAN! LET'S GO!
SORRY...
I THOUGHT I HAD THAT CLIPPED.

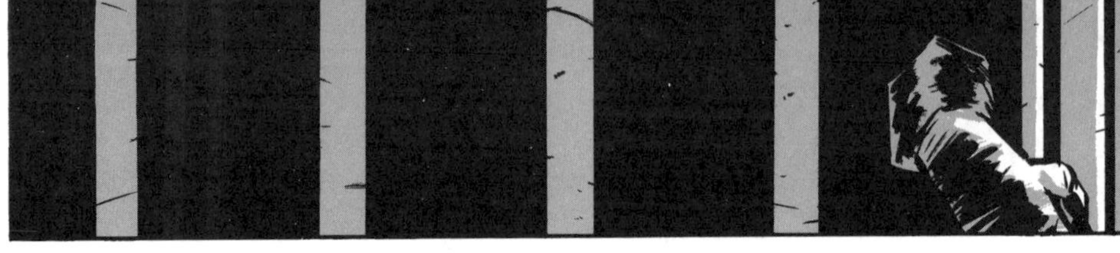

CLACK!

AW, C'MON, BABY... I'D NEVER SAY *THAT!*
YOU KNOW HOW I FEEL ABOUT YOU!

YOU SEE! ZIS ISN'T WORKING! ZEY DON'T LISTEN... SOME OF THEM ARE EVEN BORDERLINE ***BELLIGERENT!***

...ZEY ARE TOO SMART TO CONTROL, UND NOT SMART ENOUGH TO FOLLOW INSTRUCTIONS!

NONSENSE... ZEY ARE DOING BETTER ZAN EXPECTED.
THERE'S TOO MUCH PERSONALITY IN ZEM...

...ZE LITTLE ONE IS RECKLESS... ONE'S A SHOWBOAT... UND ZIS "***DR.***" WORZLE! HE IS ZE WORST OF ***ALL!***

YOU CAN SEE IN HIS EYES THAT HE UNDERSTANDS... BUT ALSO THAT HE COULDN'T CARE LESS...

IT'S INFURIATING...

HEY, MAN, WHERE AM I? *WHAT IS THIS?*

WHAT'RE YOU DOING?

BRAKA!
BRAKA!
BRAK

BANG

DO YOUR BEST TO REMEMBER ZE SEQUENCE...
...UND, NO SIGNING DURING ZE TEST!
WE WILL BE WATCHING!

WORZL

BETRÜGER.

CLICK.
ZZZZ

WUH?
EEEEEEEE
WUH!
WAH
GOLIATH
ZZZ

WHY MUST YOU ALWAYS BE SO STUBBORN!?!
CAN'T YOU SEE WHAT HAPPENS WHEN YOU DIS-OBEY ME!?!
DON'T YOU UNDERSTAND ANYZING AT ALL!?!

IF YOU DON'T UNDERSTAND YET, YOU WILL SOON...
ZZZZ

KRAK!

CLACK!

ZZZZZT
TUG
ARE YOU CRAZY?!
GET OFF OF ME!
ZZZT!
HHELL-LLP!
YOU ARE GOING TO REGRET ZIS!
I CAN PROMISE YOU!!!
ZZZZ
ZZZZ

YOU SEE! ZEY CAN'T BE CONTROLLED!
NOT LIKE ZIS!
THEIR PERSONALITIES ARE TOO DISTINCT... TOO RATIONAL!

IF WE ARE TO CONTINUE, WE HAFF TO DO IT MY WAY!
WE MUST WIPE ZE SLATE CLEAN!

KRAK!

THAK!
ALRIGHT, WORZLE... YOU'RE NEXT...
EEEEEEEEEEE

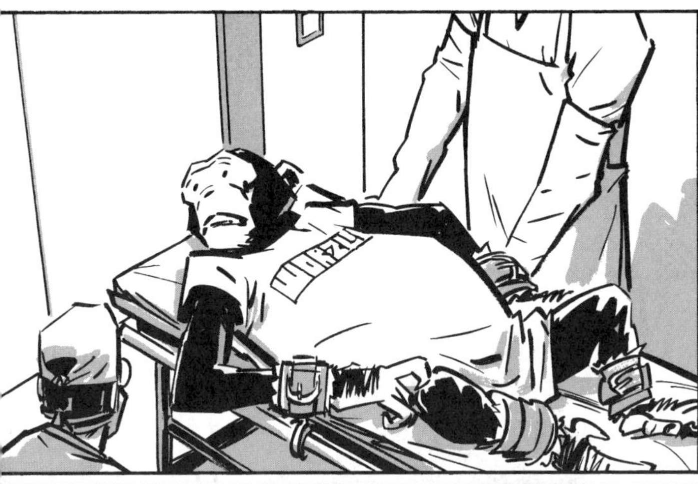

B1
B2
B3
B4
BING!

AS I PROMISED, HERR WORZLE...

NOW, PERHAPS, YOU WILL FINALLY LEARN TO DO AS YOU'RE TOLD.

ZOOOOOOOOOOOOOO-THOOM
THOOM
THOOM
THOOM
AGAIN!
THOO

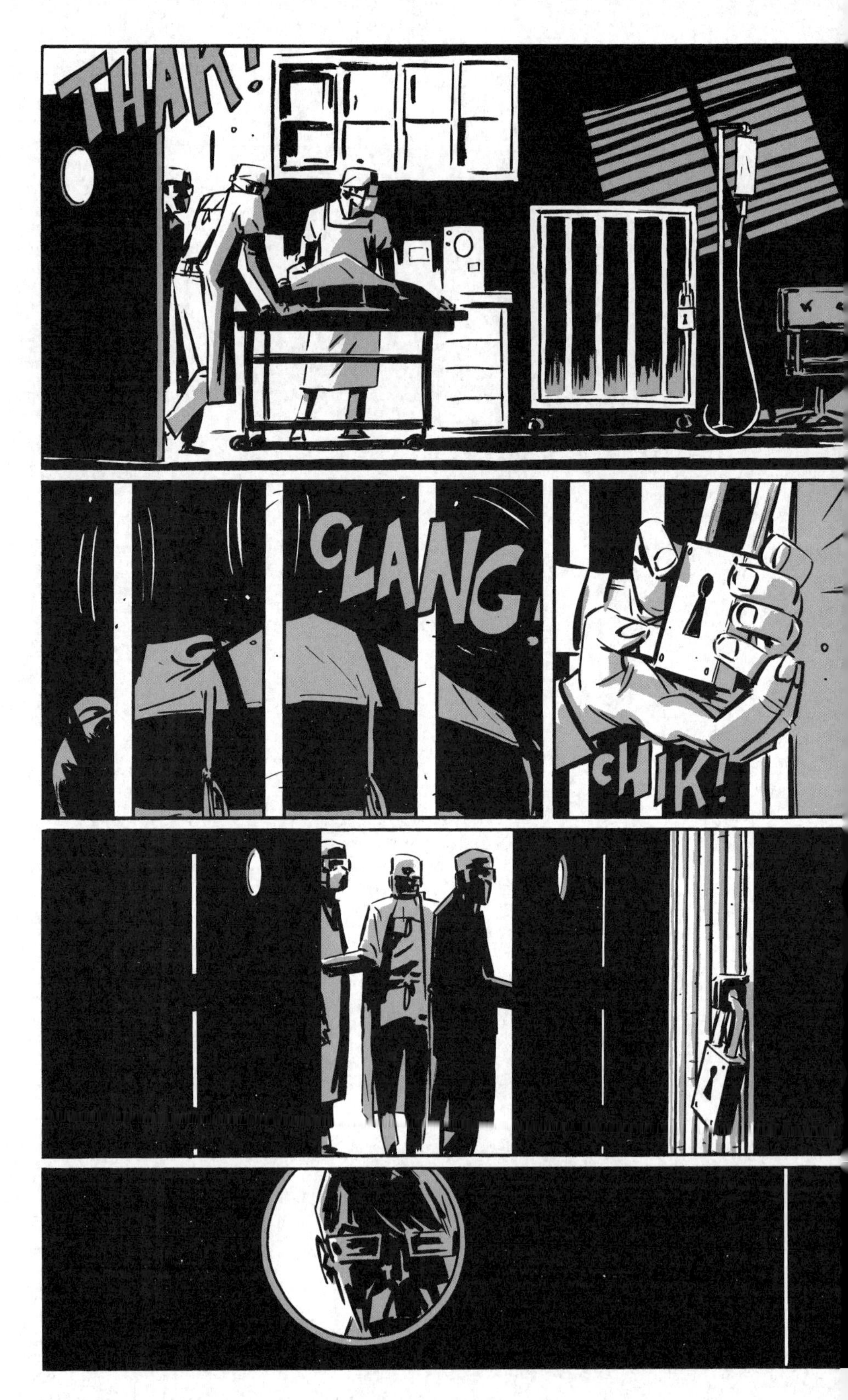
THAK!
CLANG!
CHIK!

TIC TIC TIC TIC
BLEEP
WIRRRRRRR
BEE

CLACK!

KRAK!

KAAKKOOOOOM!!

KRAK

ĐÂY LÀ NHÀ TAO... MÀY KHÔNG THUỘC VỀ NƠI NÀY...
HE SAY, "THIS HIS HOME... YOU DON'T BELONG HERE!"

WHERE'S THE BASE, GODDAMMIT?! WHERE WERE YOU TAKING THESE?!!!

TAO LÀ MỘT NGƯỜI NÔNG DÂN. TAO CHỈ ĐANG BẢO VỆ GIA ĐÌNH CỦA MÌNH MÀ THÔI.
HE SAY, "HE JUST A FARMER, PROTECTING HIS FAMILY."
YEAH, WITH *A.K.S* AND *R.P.G.S!*

ĐÂY LÀ CUỘC CHIẾN CỦA CHÚNG MÀY! CHÚNG MÀY ĐẾN ĐẤT NƯỚC CỦA TAO VÀ DẠY TAO CÁCH SỐNG Ư! BỌN MÀY ĐÚNG LÀ NHỮNG TÊN ĐẾ QUỐC BẨN THỈU!

UH... HE SAY, "THIS YOUR WAR... THAT YOU COME TO HIS COUNTRY AND TELL HIM HOW HE SUPPOSED TO LIVE..."

AND, UH... HE CALL YOU "IMPERIALIST PIG..."
WHAT...?

HOW DARE YOU, YOU MISERABLE SACK OF SHIT! MY MOMMA WAITED TABLES 'TIL SHE WAS 68!
OOF!

CAPTAIN...
...JUST GIVE ME FIVE MINUTES.
AW, CRAP... HERE WE GO...

I'LL GET WHAT YOU NEED.
HEISLER, I THOUGHT I TOLD YOU TO STAY, THE FUCK, OUTTA HERE!
HEE HEE HE

HEE HEE HEE HEE HEE HEE

THE FUCK ARE YOU LAUGHING AT NOW?
HEE HEE

THIS GENERATION PUT TOO MUCH FAITH IN POLITICS...
HEE

THE MAMA-SAN SPEAKS ENGLISH!
SON OF A...

FEELIN' TALKATIVE NOW, EH? WELL, *WHERE'S THIS FUCKIN' TRAIL LEAD? WHERE'S YOUR GOD-DAMNED BASE,* HUH!?!

LIFE USED TO BE SIMPLE... WE PROVIDED FOR THE GODS AND THEY PROVIDED FOR US...
LISTEN, YOU OLD COOT, I AIN'T INTER-ESTED IN YER WHOLE DAMN BIOGRAPHY!
...BUT THE YOUNG ONES HEARD THE STORIES ABOUT THE CITIES...

...AND THEY LEFT THE FOREST TO SEE THE CURIOSITIES.

AW, THIS IS USE-LESS!

THE MEN FROM THE CITIES SPREAD LIES WITH THEIR FORKED TONGUES...

...THEY FORGOT ABOUT THE OLD GODS AND PUT THEIR FAITH IN MAN.

...THIS WAS A TERRIBLE MISTAKE.

ALRIGHT, THAT'S ENOUGH... TELL HER TA SHUT IT...
CÂM MIỆNG NGAY, BÀ GIÀ KIA.

MAN IS PROUD OF ALL HE'S ACHIEVED... BUT HIS PRIDE CLOUDS HIS MEMORY. HE THINKS HE MADE THIS JOURNEY ON HIS OWN... THAT HE DOESN'T NEED THE GODS ANYMORE...

KRAK!
MAN DOESN'T REMEMBER THAT SHIVA IS A VENGEFUL SPIRIT...
...AND HE HAS CURSED US FOR OUR ARROGANCE!

I THOUGHT I SAW SOME-THING!
FIRST HE SENT THE *FRENCH*...
...THEN HE SENT *YOU*...
...BUT NOW...
...NOW THE *MIGHTY SHIVA* HAS LET LOOSE HIS *ARMY OF MONKEYS* TO TAKE US *ALL TO HELL!*
KA-KRAK!

WHAT DID YOU JUST SAY?
AH! YOUR FACE... THEN YOU'VE SEEN THEM!
...BUT I'VE
CAN DO.

THERE!
...SOMETHING'S MOVING DOWN THERE!

HEE HEE
I HAVE SEEN THEM...
I KNOW.
HEE HEE
HEE

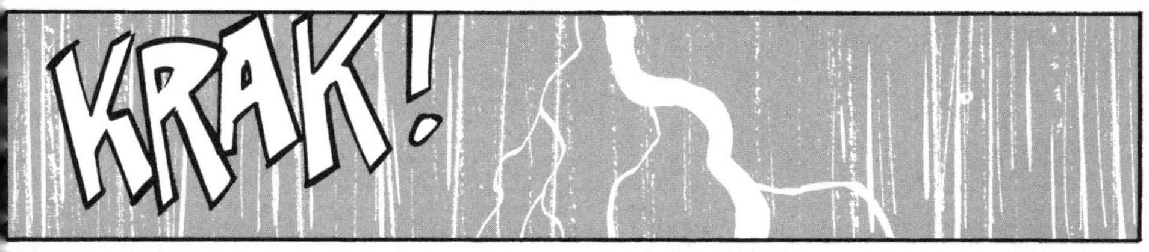
KRAK!

SHIVA'S RAGE WILL DESCEND ON US AND NOBODY WILL BE ABLE TO ESCAPE HER WRATH!

KRAKOOOM!

KRAK!

THERE! DO YOU SEE IT!?!
KRAK!
RUMMMMMMMBBBBLLLLLL
HEE HEE
YOU ARE ALL ALREADY DEAD!!!
HEE HEE

KRAK!
WE ARE ALL ALREADY DEAD!!!
HAHA HEE HEE HEE HEE HEE. HEE!

THERE! THERE HE IS!!!

BANG
HEISLER?!

WHAT THE HELL'RE YOU DOING?

WE'RE WASTING TIME.

WAAAA
WAA

EEEE!
EEEE
EEE
KA-KOOOM!

WHAT THE HELL IS WRONG WITH YOU, HEISLER?!
ZIS IS WAR, CAPTAIN!
YOU KNOW ZAT!

WE DO VHAT WE MUST.

WUHWAAH!
DOES ANYBODY ELSE HEAR THAT?
WHAT THE HELL *IS* THAT?

YOU SONUVA-BITCH!
FORGET IT, *CAP!* IT AIN'T WORTH IT!

KRAK!

WAAH!
BRRAAPPPP!
CKK... KKCCT...
WAAAH!

KRAK!

THIS AIN'T RIGHT! NONE OF THIS...
IT'S LIKE SHE SAID! THEY GONNA KILL US WHEN THEY FIND US!

WHAT THE HELL...?
WUA WAAAAAH
GO-LI-ATH!
COME BACK!
WWAAH!

KAKRAKK!!

DON'T LET THAT BITCH GET IN YOUR HEAD, EARL!
THEY'RE JUST ANIMALS!
ANIMALS!!! YOU HEAR ME!?!

POLICE
POLICE
POLICE

KKAKOOOMM!

THOOM!

BRAKA!

ZIS IS WAR, CAPTAIN!
NONE OF US ARE INNOCENT!

WUAA
WAA

HEE HEE!
HEE! HEEHEE

EEEE
EEEE
EEEEE
DOESN'T ANYBODY ELSE HEAR THAT?!
WWAAAA
KKRAK!!!

THOOM!
WAAAAAAAA
TAKKA TAKKA TAKKA!
EEEEEEEEEE

WE GOTTA GET OUTTA HERE!
NO, WAIT!
WYCKOFF'S RIGHT! I CAN HEAR THEM, TOO!
WAAAH
KKRAKK!

MY CHILDREN...
WAAAAA
KRAKK!
EEEE

KAKOOOM!!!

WAR
BRING the TROOPS HOME
GET OUT OF VIET
NO NUKES
STOP THE WAR
WUAA!
WAAH
SUCH AGONY...
I AM A MAN
I AM A MAN
KKRAAK!

KAKOOOM!!

USA
USA
USA
USA
USA
USA

WAAAAA
KRAKOOM!

WAAAAA

AHHH

RUMMMMMMMMBBBLL
WAAH!

THANK YOU, GOLIATH...

KA OOM